Hugo's Moon Crew

Written by Samantha Montgomerie

Illustrated by Maïté Schmitt

Collins

T0337548

Hugo looks up at the moon. He spots some holes.

"We could go to the moon," says Hugo.
"It would be fun."

Hugo plans a rocket. His big plan grows and grows.

Hugo gathers the crew to see the plan.
"Let's make it!" says Tulip.

The crew cuts and welds. The rocket takes shape.

Lewis and Hugo hold the ladder as Tulip screws the bolts.

Lewis polishes the windows.

Rupert makes the suits.

Tulip tops up the drinks. Ruth packs the fruit.

"Time to take off!" says Tulip. Plumes of smoke shoot out.

The crew grins as the rocket shoots off to the glowing moon.

Bump! Thump! The rocket lands on the moon. "Over there," says Hugo.

The crew follows Hugo to the holes.
They look down. "Here goes!" says Tulip
as she jumps in.

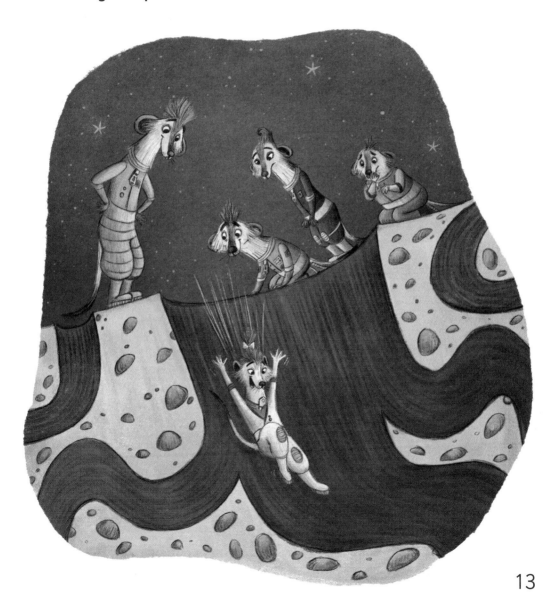

The hole leads to a tube slide! "Hugo!" says Tulip. "You should have a go!"

Hugo jumps in. He slips and slides and twists and turns to get to Tulip.

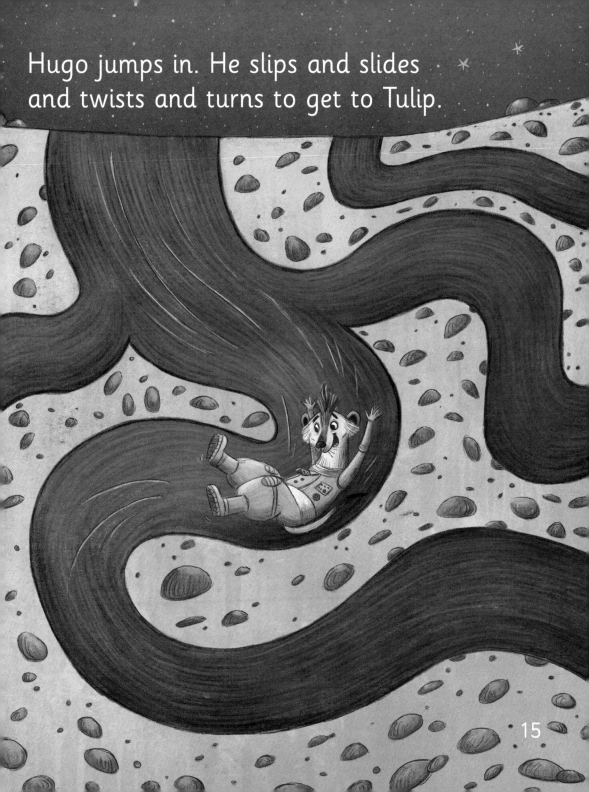

Hugo and Tulip pop up next to a cross blue
moon monster!

Lots of blue moon monsters pop up.
"Would you like to go on the tube slide?"
says Hugo.

One monster jumps down a tube. The group of blue monsters waits.

He pops back up. "You should come too!" he yells to the group.

Pop!

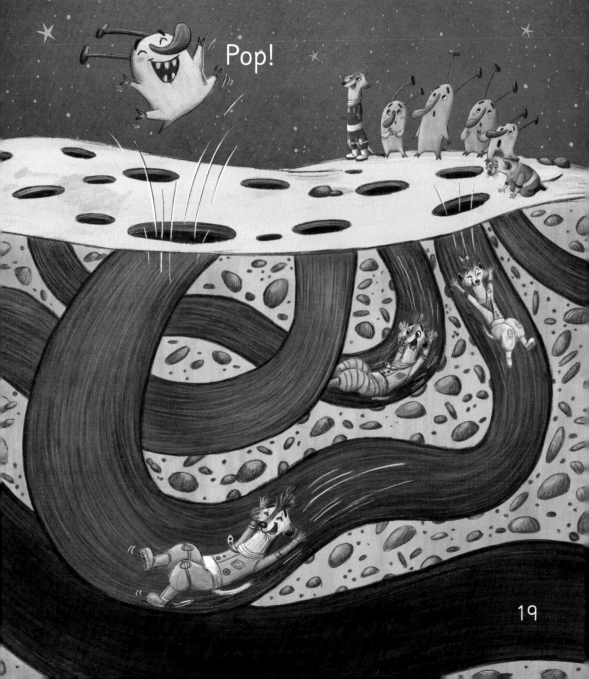

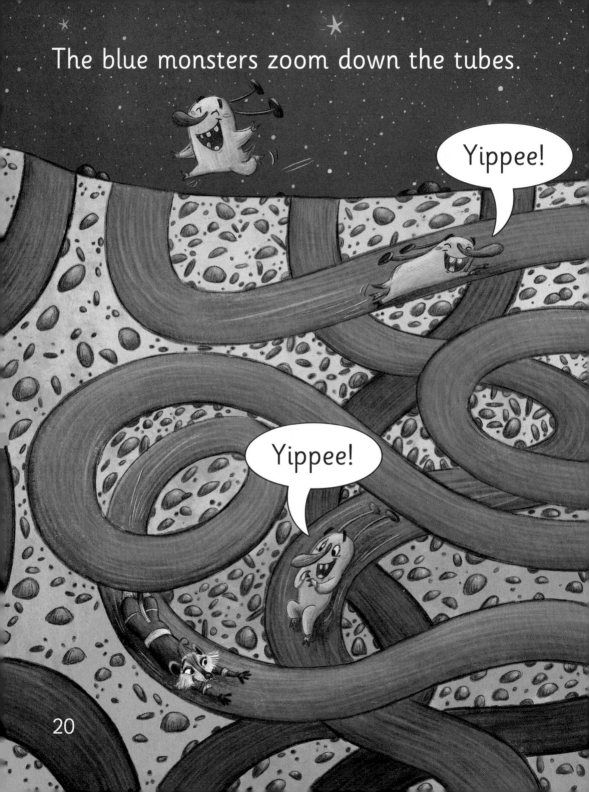

Hugo's crew shoots down the tubes, too. "Yippee," grins Hugo. "Sliding on the moon!"

21

To the moon!

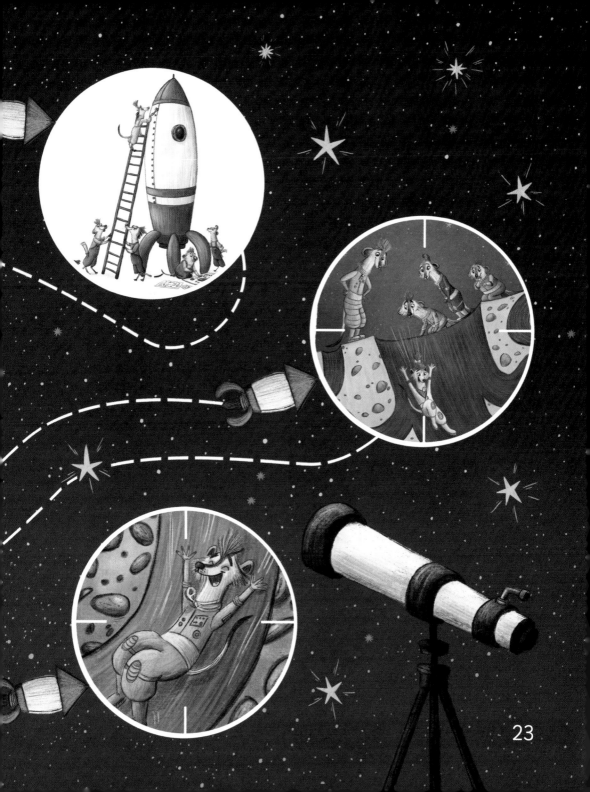

After reading

Letters and Sounds: Phase 5

Word count: 248

Focus phonemes: /ai/ ey, a-e /ee/ ea /igh/ i, i-e /oa/ o, oe, ow, o-e /oo/ ue, ui, ew, ou, u, u-e /oo/ oul

Common exception words: of, to, the, he, we, be, out, have, says, there, here, some, come, she

Curriculum links: Science: Earth and space

National Curriculum learning objectives: Reading/word reading: read accurately by blending sounds in unfamiliar words containing GPCs that have been taught; read words containing taught GPCs; Reading/comprehension: understand both the books they can already read accurately and fluently and those they listen to by checking that the text makes sense to them as they read, and correcting inaccurate reading

Developing fluency

- Your child may enjoy hearing you read the book.
- Take turns to read pages 12 and 13 with expression. Can your child make it sound as if Hugo and Tulip are really talking?

Phonic practice

- Focus on the different spellings of the long /oo/ sound.
- Look at pages 5 and 8. How many words with different /oo/ spellings can your child find? (page 5: *u – Hugo, Tulip*; *ew – crew*; page 8: *ew – Lewis*; *u – Rupert*; *ui – suits*)
- Take turns to find other /oo/ words with the same or other spellings. (e.g. *oo – shoot*; *u-e – plumes, tube*; *ou – you, group*; *ue – blue*)

Extending vocabulary

- Reread page 5 and focus on the word **says**. Discuss alternative words that could be used to show how Tulip says, "Let's make it!" (e.g. *giggles, smiles, whispers, shouts*)
- Reread page 10 and ask your child to think of a more expressive word than **says**. (e.g. *orders, calls, shouts*)
- Reread page 17 and discuss how this is a question and what could be used instead of **says**. (e.g. *asks, offers, grins*)